UNDERSTANDING
MY LIFE'S
JOURNEY

Creating and Using a Life Map for
Spiritual Growth and Personal Mission

NOEL SHERRY

To order additional copies of this book, contact:
Xlibris
844-714-8691
www.Xlibris.com
Orders@Xlibris.com

ISBN: Softcover   978-1-6698-7594-9
       EBook   978-1-6698-7593-2

Print information available on the last page

Rev. date: 04/29/2023

Introduction to "Understanding My Life's Journey" (or the Life Map Project)

This series of chapters is written to guide an adult through basic steps in creating, sharing, and using a Life Map as a tool for spiritual growth and personal mission. Ten vignettes from teachable moments in my journey will be used to illustrate each step, as I honestly share snippets of my Testimony—the title I have given to my Life Map project. Your Life Map project is best completed in a group but can be done individually—both using journaling exercises done 3 to 4 times/week over a 3-to-4-month period. The emerging field of narrative psychology refers to this practice as "Life Review," calling it a universal developmental need like learning to walk or talk. It was originally known as "spiritual autobiography" after *Confession*s--the first work of its kind written by Saint Augustine in 397 AD.

In the first chapter, I share my discovery of this ancient spiritual formation practice that has been a transformative tool for countless men and women since the time of Augustine. My discovery came during a church leadership crisis, helping me navigate a very rough transition in my life successfully. Since that time, I have had the privilege of mentoring over one hundred and fifty adults through their Life Map project, as director of Bethel Seminary of the East, New England, and the New England Christian Study Center. The impact of Life Mapping for these adults then became the focus for a Doctor in Ministry project I completed with Bethel Seminary in St. Paul, MN. That confirmed my view that this practice needs to be renewed for leaders and laypeople alike. My students were young adults at the "go-for-it" stage of life, adults in midlife transition, and seniors reminiscing on a long and productive life. Adults in all stages of life found Life Mapping to be highly beneficial, with a small percentage encountering a significant roadblock or two in their attempts to practice it.

This book has three people in view--the leader of a small group of adults working on a Life Map project, the adult who plans to create and share his or her Life Map, and the adults who will witness and support that project as it is presented. The leader needs to complete a personal Life Map before facilitating a group like this. Helps for a leader have been added at the conclusion of the series. The second chapter on life's teachable moments offers a fun starting point with some counsel on setting up the journal that will supply the raw material for a completed Life Map. The rigors of a project like this are best completed as a member of a supportive group, but chapters 3 through 7 could also guide an individual to complete a personal Life Map. In that case the selection of a mentor familiar with Life Mapping would be helpful. The biggest roadblock is addressed in the sixth chapter on overcoming the darkside in a person's life. The last three chapters address Life Map sharing for the presenter and audience (8), using a Life Map for future planning (9), and writing out a spiritual memoir from a Life Map as part one's legacy (10).

I approach Life Mapping from a distinctly Judeo-Christian point of view, though a total collection of "spiritual autobiographies" will reflect many different religious beliefs and worldview perspectives. This series could aid an adult in completing a Life Map project from any spiritual perspective. Richard Peace's helpful workbook *Spiritual Autobiography: Discovering & Sharing Your Spiritual Story* offers the following points about "noticing God," a great starting point for anyone taking up this Life Map challenge (p. 58):

> Yet there are hints of the divine in all lives: long-forgotten childhood experiences of God's presence; answers to prayer that were quickly shrugged off as "coincidence;" grace in the midst of pain; moments of joy that rush in unexpectedly; responses to nature that draw us outward; deep suspicion that maybe our mechanistic explanations of the way the universe operates are not as sound as we would like them to be; encounters with powers beyond us; worship that we did not initiate and could not contain; a sense of blessing that gives us hope and direction; a knowledge that somehow we are significant in this world. God is alive and active in the universe, and when we start to notice, it is hard to stop noticing.

ONE

Weathering a Perfect Storm at Midlife: My Discovery of Life Mapping

Midlife lived up to its reputation for me. This term was coined in 1965 to describe the transition many adults experience between ages 40 and 60. Questions about what our life-purpose is and how we have used our time thus far are often triggered in this time of self-reflection. My wife Ingelise and I were fully engaged in raising teens and caring for aging parents at age 40 when I took a position as associate pastor of a large New England congregation. After seven years of fruitful ministry, my "trigger" took the form of a church conflict that blew up into a perfect storm, leaving me in complete doubt about my calling. We were both devastated and embarked on a season of soul-searching. As should be true for people of faith, the crisis morphed into a teachable moment in which we discovered an ancient practice called "Life Mapping." The purpose of this series of chapters is to introduce the reader to this spiritual life skill and extend an invitation to engage with the simple steps I will sketch out for its practice.

The pressure cooker of ministry left precious little time for hobbies, but my teaching responsibilities gave me frequent practice with PowerPoint presentations. In the process I found a new outlet for my artistic abilities, which I have dubbed my "PowerPoint art vignettes." I have used these to illustrate life's many teachable moments. Some of them are funny, others embarrassing, many have a surprise "twist," but all of them illustrate a significant life lesson learned on my spiritual journey. Together these vignettes punctuate the chapters of my life and have become creative illustrations for sharing my Life Map with others.

This vignette depicts my discovery of Life Mapping under the mentorship Pastor Mike Bave using this life skill to help fellow pastors avoid the twin problems of cynicism and burnout. We had become friends through our town clergy group. He invited me to join his initiative authored by Robert E. Logan when he learned of my church challenges. He guided me in putting together posters for six "chapters" in my life- putting up colored sticky notes for the important persons (yellow), events (blue), and circumstances (pink) in each period. It was not long before I could write out valuable life-lessons gained in each timeframe.

Several lessons from the earliest chapter I expressed this way: "I was excited learning through God's 'Book of Nature' as a boy," and "Hearing God's 'Book of Revelation' drew me like a magnet." My young adult "conversion" as part of what has been termed "the Jesus movement" was not the only point at which God had shown up in my life. My faith crisis had temporarily hidden God's presence, but this colorful poster-display brought it into focus so I could not miss it. This was not the only aha moment Life Mapping gave to me at the time. Another lesson reminded me of the people who had invested in my life from the beginning: "My parents and other mentors, while not perfect, pointed the way."

There was an oasis for my wife and I as we wandered in our midlife dessert. A request to my church elders for a brief time of sabbatical was granted and Ingelise and I spent time in West Palm Beach where our son and daughter were enrolled in college. We connected with them, prayed, and journaled by the pool, cried and prayed some more. Spurred by emerging insights, this became a golden opportunity for growth. My anxiety and fear began to melt into gratitude, with hints of what to do going forward. But it began with a time of repentance for ways I had contributed to the conflict and what I could now do to make amends. That season of suffering birthed in me several brand-new things. I remembered an early epiphany that connected my life with the bigger story of Scripture. And I began to wrestle with my dark side that was all tangled up with PTSD from a year of combat in Vietnam, a painful chapter of my life I tried unsuccessfully to bury. Both these topics are addressed in this series on Life Map creation.

Fast forward several years and I was helping adults in two educational programs--Bethel Seminary of the East and the New England Christian Study Center--put together a Life Map as an important part of their leadership formation. Over a hundred adults took the handful of steps I will outline in this series to create and then share their stories with a group they grew to trust. I was already convinced I was on to something important, but the experience of guiding seminarians and "regular" adults surfaced some deeper questions: Why was this practice not more widely known? How is it related to the Biblical story? And can the practice be documented in the 2000 years the Church has existed? For many of my students, their Life Map learning became the highlight of their degree and course work.

A pattern began to emerge for these adults. Past conflicts of various kinds were surfaced and resolved; loved ones were consulted for their recollections; life purpose and mission were clarified; difficult transitions were smoothed out; relational bonding deepened; and a future orientation called "proflection" was fostered. It was almost as if the Life Mapping project creatively incorporated the other spiritual disciplines of prayer, Bible learning, worship, meditation, and mentoring. This practice was acting like a magnet or catalyst for renewal and faith development.

I was hooked! When the opportunity presented itself for me to complete a Doctor in Ministry program as a Bethel University employee, I jumped. And that began a deep dive on a project I titled "Life Mapping as a Means of Redemptive Transformation," which pointed me to some answers. First, I learned that Life Mapping was part of the most popular genre of literature known as autobiography. Great literature courses all agree that the "father of autobiography" is Saint Augustine (354-430 AD) who kicked off this new genre with his *Confessions*--in his case to track the movement of God's Spirit in his soul as he emerged from paganism to become a pastor and bishop. He patterned this seminal work on the Book of Psalms and the letters of the Apostle Paul, whose conversion became his inspiration. Conversion narratives patterned on Augustine now punctuate the pages of Church history. Julian of Norwich, Blaise Pascal, John Woolman, Emily Dickinson, George Washington Carver, Simone Weil, Dag Hammarskjold, and Flannery O'Connor are just a few names on a very long list.

My best Sunday School memories stem from the crazy stories told about the family tree of Abraham and Sarah. To my reasoning, Genesis pictured a very patient God. Transformation of the second and third generation after Joseph's jealous brothers sold him into slavery is a story that still brings tears to my eyes. It is my epiphany! The Hebrew word *toledoth* used 11 times in this first Biblical book as "genealogy" or "family history" refers more to the clan than to its individual members. Yet a case can be made that these accounts do resemble later spiritual autobiographies. Literary critics cite the Joseph story as one of the great moments in world literature. As Erich Auerbach has pointed out, our Old Testament heroes and heroines contrast dramatically from the ones we were assigned to read about in Homer's classic *Iliad* and *Odyssey*--remarkable for their courage and other surface attributes. The Biblical figures, in contrast, "exhibit depth, mystery, multilayeredness, a complex background, and real character development." Life Mapping aims to help us share and celebrate our stories as complex and flawed but most of all as authentic people.

Here was the biggest surprise in my research: Social science has discovered Life Mapping, too. Two facts stood out to me. Robert Butler--the first gerontologist to do research with healthy older adults in the 1950's- started out with a false assumption. The preoccupation with the past his clients seemed to display late in life did not come from decline and senility; rather, his adults were reorganizing their previous experiences with expanded understanding. He dubbed this "Life

Review" with the conclusion it is a "universal developmental need" like learning to walk and talk. Secondly, the new field of narrative psychology confirmed that even young children compile a life-story around their family attachments, saved in an autobiographical memory bank and growing like the rings on a tree. This was really striking to me: Robyn Fivush found that when parents shared adventures of their childhood and extended family around the dinner table--explaining their history through intergenerational stories--positive change and achievement for their teens rose dramatically (over those without such table conversations).

My conclusion: An important Christian discipline with echoes in Scripture and a substantial development over the past 2000 years had lapsed but was ripe for renewal. This series of chapters invites the reader to join in on the challenge, with the following steps best achieved in a supportive small group over a matter of weeks or at most a matter of months:

One   - "Weathering a Perfect Storm at Midlife" (my discovery and decision to engage in Life Mapping)

Two   - "Inspired by Life's Teachable Moments" (this step aims at "priming the pump" for this project)

Three   - "The Hinge Events that Moved Me in New Directions" (generating my Life Map outline)

Four   - "Discovering the Storyline in My Life" (tracking the plot and conflict in my story)

Five   - "Connecting My Story with a Master Story" (grounding my story in a "metanarrative")

Six   - "Redeeming the Darkside of my Life" (help from a mentor or counselor is recommended)

Seven   - "Is There an Image that 'Crowns' My Life Story?" (a creative step that helps unite my story)

Eight   - "Sharing My Life Story in a Supportive Group" (making it a witness and a blessing for others)

Nine   - "Reflecting My Story into the Future" (also known as mission, purpose, or calling)

Ten   - "Passing My Legacy to My Circle of Loved Ones" (when written out it is my spiritual memoirs)

Are you ready to take the next step? Recalling a few teachable moments from your life will start this Life Mapping journey in a fun easy way.

Another Life Lesson on my Sticky Note Timeline was this: "God went to great lengths to show this 'Prodigal Son' His grace!" Having a fellow pastor as a mentor for those first steps in Life Mapping was important. Ingelise and I were in a midlife faith crisis and my Vietnam PTSD had re-surfaced under stress. Life is messy and many of us have real trauma we drag around with us, often unconsciously. Some adults may need a counselor to "redeem the dark side" in their lives. It is well worth the effort. Now I am a mentor for others, calling interested adults to consider the exciting Life Map challenge. This discipline is not just for pastors or seminarians. It is equally relevant to the young adult at the "go-for-it" stage of life, the mid-lifer in need of course correction, or the senior wondering about legacy. One of my favorite verses in the Bible touches on the theme of creation: "LORD, you are our father. We are the clay, and you are our potter; we are all the product of your labor" (Isaiah 64:8). Life Mapping has the potential for "cracking open" this mysterious dialog with the divine Potter. In my time of need I never imagined this would become an important part of God's purpose and calling for my life. And there was this immediate bonus: Our renewal led directly to some measures of restoration in the Church family after the storm.

TWO

*Inspired by Life's Teachable Moments:
Second Step in a Life Mapping Project*

I will never forget that glance in my boyhood when I walked in my front door with a Nazi war helmet on and met my father's eye. He was a World War II veteran who used this as a "teachable moment" to set his son strait. Remembering experiences like this was one of the first fruits of my Life Map work. This series of chapters on Life Mapping--also known as "spiritual autobiography"--invites the reader to consider taking up this time-honored practice. In my first chapter, I shared my discovery of the practice during a midlife faith crisis, with ways it became a blessing in disguise for my wife Ingelise and I. I went from doubting my pastoral calling to finding a brand-new purpose going forward. This second chapter in the series offers readers a fun way to begin putting together their own Life Map, "priming the pump" by remembering and recording a variety of teachable moments in a journal.

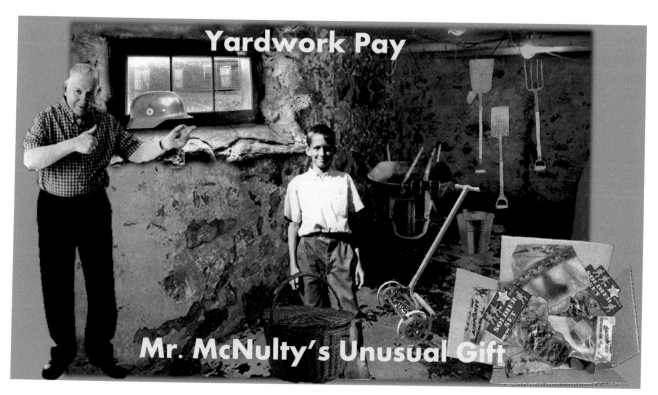

Yardwork Pay

Mr. McNulty's Unusual Gift

This second vignette created with my PowerPoint art tells the story of how that war helmet got on my head. A Mr. McNulty employed us neighborhood kids to do his yardwork, cutting the lawn, pulling weeds, raking leaves. He kept a large cardboard box in his basement garden room stocked with plastic toys from the company he worked for. At the end of our chores, he invited us in to pick out a water gun, a plastic doll, or something else. One Saturday he noticed my interest in an old war helmet collecting dust on the windowsill. Well, that became my yardwork pay, setting me up for that confrontation with my father. After demanding I remove it in a loud voice, my dad sat me down and explained how Hitler had plunged the world into a devastating war just before I was born, murdering six million Jewish people as the pinnacle of his many war crimes. I was stunned. It took me years to process that brief father-son talk. And I never saw that helmet again.

While the phrase "teachable moment" first appeared in a 1917 book, we need to credit Moses with the important notion behind it. Just before he breathed his last, he stood with the elders of Israel atop Mount Nebo surveying the land on the opposite side of the Jordan River valley. The Lord had promised to give this parcel as an inheritance to the people descended from Abraham and Sarah. Pressing upon Moses was how the faith that accompanied that inheritance would be passed on to the next generations. In that moment of gravity, I see Moses sweeping his shepherd's staff across the arc of that western horizon, with these words: "Love the Lord your God with all your heart and with all your soul and with all your strength. These commandments that I give you today are to be upon your hearts. Impress them on your children. Talk about them when you sit at home and when you walk along the road, when you lie down and when you get up" (Deuteronomy 6:5-7). "Impress" is one of about 20 Biblical words for teaching or learning, this verb literally meaning "to pierce." Teachable moments will pop up each day, he urged, with their guided conversations aimed at internalizing the great truths of the faith. And thus, this metaphor of carefully aiming an arrow at a target's bullseye was applied to parental teaching.

A human development expert named Robert Havihurst popularized this phrase in 1952 when he referred to a "teachable moment" as the time when a person is primed to learn a new task. He arranged a chronological list of "developmental tasks" from the cradle to the grave--like finding a mate or parenting children. A prior task must be mastered before we are ready to learn the next, he asserted. Parents and teachers jumped on the idea to describe a child's readiness to learn, his or her natural curiosity, or anything that spurs a novel discovery. My "Yardwork Pay" incident fits the latter category. Like a dark cloud that cast a shadow on an otherwise happy childhood, my father's words drilled deep down into my life. This became a kind of *crossroads moment* for me, a quest to find out how (and why) the world was so broken. The shadow reached all the way to high school when I read and wrote a report on Hitler's autobiographical rant *Mein Kampf*, German for "My Struggle," trying to grasp what would dredge up such depravity.

The adults I mentored on their Life Mapping project for Bethel Seminary of the East and the New England Christian Study Center shared many teachable moments during their preparation, most of them light-hearted and humorous. Each student kept a notebook or secure digital journal for this introductory Spiritual Formation course, using Richard Peace's practical workbook *Spiritual Journaling* to track their personal reflections. Sharing a variety of teachable moments bonded the group together, raised anticipation, and built the trust needed for the endgame--Life Map sharing.

The "deliverable" for this second step in Life Map creation is simply to record a variety of teachable moments from the reader's life story. Three would be perfect. A brief prayer requesting God's help in recall is a good starting point, settled in some quiet space with a journal. Narrative psychologist

Dan McAdams offers good advice on variety. He introduced the "Life Story Interview" in 1995, interviewing hundreds of adults for eight kinds of critical or key events--including a *peak* and *"nadir"* experience (high and low point); *a turning point*; the *earliest memory*, and an important childhood, adolescent, and adult incident which had real impact on the direction their life has taken.

A word of advice on what to include and what to leave out: A later step will address "redeeming the darkside of my life," so set your *low point* aside for now. A key moment that should be included in this exercise (with several of the teachable moments already mentioned) Peace called *"the hinge event."* The next step for Life Map creation is titled "the Hinge Events that Moved Me in New Directions," because the recall and arrangement of these in your life will generate the outline for your life story. A hinge event could be a move to a new place, a new venture, a new commitment, a new person in your life, or a major challenge, change, or loss. Here is a journaling prompt, questions for you to respond to:

- What is the *hinge event* that set the current chapter of my life in motion?
- When did this *hinge event* happen? What title would I give to this chapter of my life?
- How did this impact me? What am I learning about myself as a result?
- What relationships have been primary? What emotions have I experienced?

Mr. McNulty never asked me what happened to the Nazi war helmet he gave me as pay for yardwork. Nor was he aware that his souvenir signaled for me a detour on an unsettling *crossroads* with uncomfortable questions like the following: Given the right (or wrong) conditions, could any one of us fall into a moral black hole? That was a fear that I think steered me onto a Judeo-Christian path. My Life Map work brought this teachable moment right to the surface because it also became a *hinge event* for a new chapter in my life which I titled "A Dark Cloud Over My Childhood." That was 1956--just a year before the launch of Sputnik by the Soviet Union (October 4, 1957). Interestingly, I now trace several commitments back to this *hinge event*. I have come to count many Jewish people as my friends. I would never apply the word "Holocaust" to anything other than its first meaning. And I have become a staunch advocate fighting all forms of antisemitism. Life has many twists and turns. Have fun journaling!

THREE

The Hinge Events that Moved Me in New Directions: Third Step in a Life Mapping Project

Anyone born before 1950 will remember the event captured here with a vignette I titled "TV Draft Lottery." The date was December 1, 1969 and I was glued to CBS TV with a nervous audience of draft-age adults. America had recently elected its 46th President, Richard M. Nixon, on his promise to extract us from the unpopular conflict in Southeast Asia. The war had taken a heavy toll on all branches of the service, and Uncle Sam desperately needed fresh recruits! Roger Mudd's voice from Selective Service headquarters in DC preempted Mayberry RFD: "Good evening, tonight for the first time in 27 years the United States has again started a draft lottery." Word on the street had anyone with a DOB in the first 190 picks as Vietnam-bound. I was on the edge of my seat. And this was the "hinge event" that ushered me into a new Chapter of life. This series invites readers to engage in a time-honored practice called "Life Mapping," with this chapter a guide to a third step--generating a Life Map outline from a list of hinge events that have moved me in new directions.

One: Journaling a List of My Hinge Events

I can remember riding a hinged door as a young boy, a habit my parents frowned on. Hinges join important furniture parts together, with another connotation for the word being "turning point." Hinge events are turning points or transitions when life moves us in a new direction. These need not be dramatic--like a family move to a new home, a new step in our education, or a new person or commitment in our life. On the other hand, a traumatic incident, religious experience, or world-shaping event like 9-11 could signal a dramatic shift in the direction my life takes. This step invites the reader to record all the hinge events he or she can recall in a journal. For now, just relax in a quiet space, suspend evaluation, and simply respond to the question: "What are the hinge events in my life?"

Many people have no experience keeping a journal, so why is this important? John Calvin began his influential work *Institutes of the Christian Religion*, with the important truth that wisdom has two parts--knowledge of God and knowledge of self. The Bible offers a guide to the former, a personal journal is key to the latter. Knowing who we are now or who we will become, like the rings of a tree, form around who we were as a child, a teen, and a young adult. Journaling will recover each of these "rings" or life-Chapters. Richard Peace refers to this as a "spiritual" journal:

> By reviewing our past, we also begin to recognize the footprints of God in our life. They weren't always clear at the time, but in retrospect we can see patterns. We come to understand how God was at work, shaping us in unique ways. And so we understand our story from a spiritual--as well as historical--point of view.

My "TV Draft Lottery" vignette was just one of the hinge events I wrote down in my journal. My young adult time had a cluster of hinge events, so I recorded them all--getting wounded on a last patrol in Vietnam, emergency medical care at Walson Army Hospital in New Jersey, meeting my wife-to-be Ingelise, and inviting Jesus to be Lord of my life. This part of the assignment was a lot of fun for me. After a hesitant start, the ideas started to flow faster than I could get them on paper, a long list of hinge events from birth to present, in no particular order. And I discovered that prayer settled my mind and aided in recall of hinges I had long forgotten.

Two: Using My Hinge Events to Form Life-Chapters

This next part of the exercise was a little more challenging for me, arranging my long list of hinge events in chronological order and deciding which of the events formed distinct "Chapters" in my story. For many of us the past has become murky and mysterious. For some there are broken relationships or painful memories we would rather forget. All of this was true for me, so I found hope and help from Dr. Ira Progoff, facilitator of the popular Journaling Workshops. He suggested we treat our past not as one big whole but as a series of interconnected periods or parts, each with its own distinct character. In this way we will get to know our history from an internal point of view, discerning what the people, events, ideas, and emotions meant for each "Chapter" included in the timeline.

Putting my hinge events in chronological order took a little bit of time. I consulted some resources I had on hand--a yearbook, an old scrapbook, and a resume. I asked my parents and brothers about several of the events and dates. My wife Ingelise had become an excellent scrapbooker, so she helped with final arrangement of the hinge events on a timeline. A side benefit I had not anticipated was that my project picked up the interest of my extended family and friends. Forming the Chapters for my Life Map from this timeline of hinge events turned out to be much easier than I thought it would be. Some of the hinge events jumped out and became the beginning (or endpoint) for a Chapter, others blended in with the contents of the Chapter. Organizing this outline for my Life Map was most satisfying, not unlike the feeling of joy I had at getting my first school term paper organized into a good outline.

For illustration, "TV Draft Lottery" clearly marked the beginning of a new Chapter I titled "Caught by the Draft," addressing my two years of service with the US Army. This Chapter began on December 1, 1969, the date of that infamous televised event. The other important hinges from this eventful Chapter--getting wounded, recovery, meeting Ingelise—then gave to this fifth Chapter of my Life Map its character as a time of change and discovery. In just two short years, I nearly lost my leg, found God, met my wife-to-be, and "found myself!" Indeed, my lowest and highest points in life were here. The only question to settle now was when this Chapter ended? Technically, my Purple Heart ended my military service, but the next Chapter did not really begin until I verbalized what I call my "skeptic's prayer," the night before inviting Jesus to be my commanding officer. I vividly remember when that happened, December 22nd, 1971: "God, I don't even know your name, but if You are listening, I am ready to turn to you for help." That hinge marked a new Chapter I titled "Caught Up in the Jesus Movement."

The adults I had the privilege of mentoring on Life Map creation at Bethel Seminary of the East and the New England Christian Study Center had fun with this step in the process. They found that it took a project that at first seemed like a mountain and made it into a manageable mole hill. Once they journaled their hinge events and generated the Chapters for an emerging Life Map, I assigned them the task of naming each chapter with a descriptive or humorous title. That kept the project moving forward. One word of caution: Some of my mentees were tempted to mark new chapters using every hinge event in their journal, ending up with too many Chapters to fit into a Life Map presentation. My rule of thumb: 6 to 12 chapters is manageable, so a 45-minute presentation will allow 4 to 5 minutes per Chapter.

Three: Exploring Each Chapter Using a Set of Questions

This is where a Life Mapper begins to "put meat on the bones" of his or her outline. My advice was to select any one of the Chapters as a starter, penning to the prompt "it was a time when…" I found the following questions from Peace's *Spiritual Journaling* more than adequate to describe the character of each chapter:

- When did this Chapter begin? Describe the boundary or hinge event that kicked it off…
- Who were the key people in your life during this Chapter and what role did they play?
- What were the key concepts that marked this Chapter and what were you interested in?
- What responsibilities did you have and how did you spend your time?
- What was your spiritual and emotional life like and how was God present to you?
- What was your physical state--were you healthy or challenged in physical ways?

I was surprised at how my journal filled up as I used these questions to tackle each Chapter I had dated and given a title to. The twelve Chapters that first formed my Life Map had from 2 to 4 pages scribbled out detailing what I now recalled. While I had followed directions to suspend judgement earlier in the process, this step invited me to evaluate what I was learning and how I was maturing as a person.

Narrative psychologists call this Life Review and include it as an essential developmental task, not unlike learning to manage our emotions or get along with others. Now in my seventies, I have two new Chapters under my belt--one involving "downsizing" and the other "retirement," the quotation marks qualifying just how positive these Chapters have been. Interestingly, my Life Mapping practice became a huge plus for taking the sting out of both challenging transitions. For a third journaling session, take your most recent life Chapter and respond to these six questions. This will become a pattern for journaling all your life Chapters as you prepare a Life Map presentation.

Shortly after receiving my low draft number in the national lottery, a friend tried to talk me into joining him in paying a NYC psychiatrist $75 for a note that freed him from the draft. Today I contemplate how different my life story would have been if I had joined draft dodgers on a trek that often led to Mexico or Canada. That is a crossroads I am glad I did not take. On the eve I offered up my post-Vietnam skeptic's prayer, my life was sad. The future appeared bleak. The self-focus of hippy ideals had blind-folded and spun me on a downward spiral. I had reached the bottom and needed help. And I had no idea the conflict in my life was about to change dramatically. Which leads to the next or fourth step for the Life Mapper, "Discovering the Storyline in My Life." It turns out that narrative theory or parsing a good story can richly reward anyone on this reflective journey.

FOUR

Discovering the Storyline in My Life: A Fourth Step in Life Mapping

After dropping out of Rensselaer Polytechnic Institute in Troy, NY, I rented a house with a couple of buddies on State Route Nine, just above the Latham Circle. One day we debated the question of whether a person is more creative under the influence of marijuana, or less so. As passionate converts to the Sixties' social revolution, this seemed to be an article of faith. We thus planned a "psychedelic experiment" to settle the question, purchasing sheets of parchment paper and readying the large selection of oil paints stacked on basement shelves. Friday came and contrary to former President Bill Clinton's claim, we did inhale. We then immersed ourselves in "the experiment," taking breaks only for munchies.

I remember a smudge in the middle of my sheet, which in my state of mind morphed into a very distinct head of Jesus. Under my brush this became Christ crucified in a deeply conflicted world wheeling its way through time. We crashed and rose the next morning to check our hypothesis. The consensus was unanimous on a low creativity rating for their paintings. Turning to my work of art, one exclaimed, "Holy cow, Noel, you met God last night!" My other buddy added, "I'm callin' ya 'Pastor' from now on." And so began a strange new metamorphosis in my life!

My generation came of age in the Sixties, shaped in no small way by the assassination of President John F. Kennedy on November 22nd, 1963. As a "counterculture," we questioned almost everything--from the ethics of the Vietnam war to the efficacy of civil rights legislation at countering rampant racism. I was in rebellion against the organized religion I had been brought up with at Chatterton Hill Congregational Church in White Plains, N.Y. This became my cultural setting, and it formed a tumultuous plot-conflict that bound me up in a tight knot. This fourth chapter will guide the reader participating in the Life Map project in tracing the storyline in his or her life.

In preparation for this step in the readers' Life Map work, it will be helpful to explore one of the greatest stories ever narrated--first for the elements it shares with all stories (in *italics*) and then for what literary expert Leland Ryken attributed its matchless status to. The family I grew up in as one of four boys was notorious for sibling rivalry, but we pale in comparison to the family dysfunction described in Genesis chapters 37 through 50. In brief, the family history of Joseph offers a detailed *character* study of this fourth patriarch in a Genesis epic story caught in a *plot* that ended well, as all *comic* tales do. Fourth-generation Joseph found himself in a tragic *setting* in which his older brothers scapegoated him for their father Jacob's favoritism, symbolized by a special gift--a prized "coat of many colors" (37:3). Joseph's eleven brothers become insanely jealous as their younger brother related dreams about his destiny as the future family leader, plotting murder but settling for the sale of their brother into Egyptian slavery for 20 shekels of silver (37:28).

As the *conflict* intensified, Joseph suffered one adversity after another through no fault of his own, the narrator repeating a major Genesis *theme*, God's covenant love: "The LORD was with Joseph and showed him mercy" (39:21). *Tested* as it were by fire, Joseph's moral *choices* lead the reader to the breathtaking *climax* of the story. Years have passed and the tables have turned. "Emotional voltage" peaks for the reader, comments Ryken, because we know Joseph's destiny as family leader, but his brothers do not. Father Jacob believes his son is dead, proven by the animal blood his brothers soaked the special coat in years earlier (37:33). Our *protagonist's* unique gift for interpreting dreams gained his release from prison and appointment to high office after Joseph convinced the Pharoah his dreams were warnings of a devastating famine to come (41:25).

When Joseph's brothers appeared before their disguised brother begging for food, he devised a series of *moral tests* to ascertain whether they had changed their ways. The impassioned plea of older brother Judah in chapter 44 persuaded him they had undergone an authentic *character transformation*--the occasion for his shocking *revelation*: "I am Joseph your brother... Now, do not be upset and do not be angry with yourselves because you sold me here, for God sent me ahead of you to preserve life" (45:4-5)! The story's *resolution* pictures the unlikely healing and reunion of a family that should have self-destructed years earlier. By the end of the story, the reader knows that God's covenant love has facilitated a genuine miracle! Joseph's embrace of his brothers and his aged father after years of estrangement puts an exclamation point on this gem of a story.

Ryken pointed out the distinct "U-shape" of the Joseph story which takes the reader down through tragedy and suffering, and then up to a surprising transformation. As part of the epic genre of Genesis, the Joseph story is much more than mere *comedy*, it is part of what philosopher's label "metanarrative" --a story incorporating everyone and everything and claiming to make sense out of all reality. Ryken expressed it forcefully:

> It is a moderately long story that traces the early ancestry of a nation. Because of the covenant theme that pervades the story, it is a story of destiny. This is much more than the history of individual heroes [Abraham, Isaac, Jacob, Joseph] or even of a family; it is nothing less than the beginning of salvation history, the history of the whole human race viewed from the perspective of God's acts of redemption and judgement (pp. 80-81).

The deeper metanarrative conflict for Joseph and his family was the polytheism the ancient world was awash in, with grim means of reaching out for divine favor--the human sacrifice of Abraham's city of origin (Ur) or the cult of sacred prostitution practiced where he settled his family (Canaan). The covenant relationship revealed in Genesis (and the rest of the Bible) was a radical new idea for divine connection unveiled by Hebrew monotheism. Indeed, part of the uniqueness of this story is that God Himself is present as a decisive difference-maker, the "hidden" *Protagonist*, as it were.

My journey in life (and Life Map project) shares some common elements with the Joseph story, such as *setting*, *plot*, *conflict*, *testing*, *climax*, *resolution*, and *character transformation*. The "knot" I was tied up in as a young adult had to do with the deeper metanarrative conflict in my modern cultural setting. James Sire described three worldviews that have been part of my life's journey. *Naturalism* is summed up in Carl Sagan's famous statement, "The Cosmos is all that is or ever was or ever will be." I swallowed that idea whole, discarding my Sunday School faith. Without God in the picture, my emerging identity formed around Jean Paul Sartre's *Existentialism*: "At first, he [man] is nothing, only afterwards will he be something, and he himself will have made him what he will be." My participation in this brave new world soon collapsed around me. With the Beatles I turned to Eastern *Pantheism* for grounding in something beyond myself. That did not resolve my metanarrative *conflict*. My students at Bethel Seminary of the East, in presenting their Life Maps, shared plot-conflicts borne of four more metanarratives on Sine's worldview list--*Deism*, *Nihilism*, *New Age*, and *Postmodernism*.

The following prompts are offered to help the Life Mapper discern the storyline unfolding in his or her life. Write down your responses to each question in your journal, setting aside about a half hour to do it. Be open to the possibility that this assignment may generate some changes on your Chapter timeline:

- Describe the *plot conflict* you have experienced life...are there any "metanarrative" dimensions to that *conflict* that this chapter helped you to recall?
- How would you describe the *physical setting* you grew up in, including a brief portrait of your family of origin? What was the center of warmth in the home you grew up in?
- Describe the set of beliefs, attitudes, and customs that were part of the *cultural setting* you grew to maturity in...Who most embodied these and how were they taught or communicated?
- In what ways would you say your *character* was shaped or developed? Was there a particular experience or challenge that *tested* your character in a significant way? How did you react?
- Is there a specific crossroads event in which you had to make a *decision* or *choice*? Why did you move in the direction that you did? What might have unfolded if you had chosen the alternative?
- If you had to describe the *climax* of your life to date, what would it be? Can you speak of a particular *resolution* to the conflict that has driven the plot in your life story?

The last question points up one of the unique differences between a Life Map and the Joseph story. Most obvious is the "auto" in autobiography--which means I am both subject and narrator of my own story. Just as obvious, I have no idea how my story will turn out in the end! It is I who decide on point-of-view, choice of episodes, and a unifying theme that holds all the Chapters in my story together. Unity in the Joseph story is achieved by the narrator in two ways, by the hero's quest to fulfill his destiny (announced right at the beginning) and by putting the theme-- the victory of redemptive suffering over intended evil--in the main character's own words. Unity for this project emerges as the Life Mapper journals through each chapter identified in the third step, "The Hinge Events that Moved Me in New Directions," with my suggestion he or she journal through one Chapter per week using the set of questions included there, until the journal holds my whole life-to-date expressed in words.

Narrative psychologist Robert Coleman offered criteria for a "successful" Life Review, another name for a Life Map. One of these is "truth value" or authenticity, which simply means telling the truth as I know and have experienced it. It is one factor that makes autobiography the most popular genre in literature. The next or fifth step in this project will be "Connecting My Story in with a Master Story." The Judeo-Christian Scriptures (of which the Joseph story is a part), has become my Master Story. My vignette for this chapter captures one scene in the major *plot conflict* of my life--experimenting with a Hippy lifestyle and one of its "sacraments." Reflecting on how this *tested* my character, I can see myself now at that crucial 1968 *crossroads*--taking a sharp spiritual turn. I was one of many in the late Sixties initiated into what has been called "the Jesus Movement," sharing this strange new metamorphosis. This has become the real *climax* in my life story, a *resolution* to the turmoil that had me bound up in a tight knot.

FIVE

Connecting My Story in with a Master Story: Fifth Step in Life Mapping

Mamie Lou Roots was a neighbor of my family in White Plains, New York, where I grew up. Her husband Logan had served as a medical missionary in Vietnam--formerly Indochina--and reportedly, had saved the life of Communist dictator Ho Chi Minh. I was a frequent guest in their home, and she was my fifth grade Sunday School teacher. Our class made up mostly of boys met in Chatterton Hill Congregational Church's downstairs "dungeon," and I am sure she struggled with how to keep our attention as she told the stories of Old Testament heroes and heroines assigned in her teacher's guide. Mischievous boys, a dank basement, and a dry curriculum were all challenges, but something happened in that setting that I will never forget. I was drawn into the Biblical story of Joseph in such a way that even today its narration moves me to tears. This vignette recreates the scene as I remember it and this fifth chapter in my series aims to help the reader engaged in Life Mapping to connect his or her story in with a metanarrative. Mine became "the Master Story" of Scripture.

I have asked myself what it was about a Sunday School lesson that would move a ten-year-old boy to tears in front of his peers? I think the first thing was the sibling rivalry in the Joseph narrative, jealous brothers selling their father's favorite son into slavery. I had siblings, three brothers, and we had more than our share of rivalry--such as the time I played football with my older brother Burt and he tackled me on our hardwood floor, chipping my front teeth. But Burt never disowned me. That extreme act in a very dysfunctional family drew me further into this ancient tale recorded in Genesis chapters 37 through 50. I remember putting myself in Joseph's shoes, wondering what would happen to him in Egypt, marveling that he handled servitude, false accusation, and imprisonment with such grace and skill. The only explanation the narrator offered was that "God was with him and showed him mercy" (39:21).

But it was the climax of the story that moved me to the core, when a severe famine brought Joseph's treacherous brothers before him in Egypt to beg for food, totally unaware the official they petitioned was the one they betrayed years earlier. Interpreting Pharoah's disturbing dreams seemed to me the perfect plot twist that would promote a prisoner into a ruling position. I was on Joseph's side as he put his brothers through severe testing, both of us finally convinced they had learned their lesson. And then the great reveal: "I am Joseph your brother... Now, do not be angry with yourselves because you sold me here, for God sent me ahead of you to preserve life" (45:4-5). The miracle of that moment became my epiphany. This had to be God! For only He could turn a total tragedy into an unforgettable comedy--crowned with forgiveness and a celebratory family reunion!

In my survey of spiritual autobiographies, I made a remarkable discovery: I am not unique, for countless men and women have had similar encounters with Scripture. Saint Augustine (354-430 AD) pointed to the Apostle Paul's dramatic conversion as the pattern for sharing his life-story in *Confessions*. In her autobiography--the first in the English language--Marjory Kempe (1373-1438) envisioned herself present at the birth and crucifixion of Jesus. John Bunyan (1628-1688) saw himself reenacting the whole Gospel drama in *Grace Abounding to the Chief of Sinners*. John Woolman (1720-1772) envisioned a Black man created in God's image, exactly as he, calling him to a lifelong mission to eliminate slavery. The most vivid example I found was the case of one Johann Georg Hamann (1730-1788), who narrated his own redemptive transformation while "putting himself into" the Genesis account of Cain and Abel:

> I recognized my own crimes in the history of the Jewish people ... on the evening of the 31st of March I read the fifth chapter of Deuteronomy and fell into deep thought. I thought of Abel, of whom God said (Genesis 4:11), "The earth has opened her mouth to receive thy brother's blood." I felt my heart thump. ... All at once I felt my heart swell, and pour out in tears, and I could not longer--I could not longer conceal from my God that I was the brother murderer, the murderer of his only-begotten Son.

What is it about the Bible that gives it this transformative character for readers? Literary critic Northrop Frye offered one solid clue. Early societies like that of Joseph's depended upon word-of-mouth for daily communication, with some of their oral stories rising to a new status as "meta-stories." These gave the group the "inside story" on their reason-for-being, their values and beliefs. "They thus become 'sacred' as distinct from 'profane' stories, and form part of what the Biblical tradition calls revelation." A modern equivalent for this is a "worldview," answering the fundamental questions of human existence, such as where we come from, what's wrong and what the solution is, and where we are headed. Postmodernism, probably the most influential worldview today, has coined the term "metanarrative" for this, what is also called the "Master Story" or "Grand Narrative" of Scripture. Postmodernists are skeptical of all metanarratives, favoring the smaller individual stories that make up our lives.

Some have even compared the Bible to a Shakespearean play with an audience call to participate in and complete the action in the last act. Two commentators have interpreted the Master Story as a six-act drama, each beginning with a "C'" word-- the *creation*, the *chaos* of the Fall, God's *covenant* with Israel, the redemptive work of *Christ*, the birth of the *Church*, and the *consummation* that completes the drama. These six movements are "all dramatized as a king who established a kingdom, lost it, and then regained it again" (Bartholomew & Goheen). The Biblical drama presumes a "backstory," too, in which Lucifer--archangel of light and wisdom--failed in his frontal assault against God, but then retaliated by alienating God's Beloved (Adam and Eve) in the Garden of Eden, setting in motion the redemptive drama our race is still engaged in. Ideally, each of us will track with several of these great themes in our own journey. Augustine, Kempe, Bunyan, Woolman, and Hamaan, were profoundly impacted by at least one of these themes. For me it was *Covenant*--God's covenant love for Joseph and his broken family. But I can reflect on how each one of the themes has impacted me in some significant way.

Another question pops up regarding metanarrative. How exactly does the Master Story become the key or integrative factor in my "small" story? Here there are many possibilities, each of us being as unique as our fingerprint. It is instructive to name several ways this spiritual transformation takes place. Consider the following list offered by Robert Brown: The Biblical Story becomes mine...

- by showing its compelling power in relation to my story;
- by being retold to me or by me in various ways;
- by becoming relevant and personal to me as a testimony to one of its key themes;
- as I reenact this Master Story at the communion table (or in a Passover seder);
- by having it convict me of sin (the way David was by the prophet Nathan in 2 Samuel 12);
- by releasing me from the distortion or delusion of competing narratives or worldviews.

One thing is certain. Without being anchored in a metanarrative, my story is likely to be fragmentary and disconnected. Narrative Psychology offers a key finding in this regard. In a major study of Israeli and Palestinian youth, it was discovered that each group formed its identity from very different metanarrative stories--resulting in redemption stories for the Israelis and "stories of contamination and tragedy" for the Palestinian teens (P. L. Hammack). Metanarrative really matters!

Now for the journal exercise: Set aside a block of time to respond to the following questions, adding any new insights you surface to the Chapters of your life you have already journaled:

- Can you recall an epiphany in which God became real to you?
- Describe God's Presence in your life (after reviewing each of the Chapters journaled so far) ...
- Which of the six themes mentioned here touch on and impact your life story?
- Specifically, how would you describe your relationship with Christ (or with a Master Story)?
- How has God's Master Story (or an alternative metanarrative) helped you to make sense of the past, present, and future?

Journaling my past has made me acutely aware of the teachable moments when God became real and present to me. My epiphany in the Joseph story is certainly the deepest and most emotional of these experiences, with "epiphany" rooted in a Greek word for "striking appearance." I can name a handful of precious people God used to point me to His Master Story, including an Army medic and chaplain who witnessed to their faith in Jesus under combat conditions. While not everyone has a dramatic conversion experience, mine did involve a radical turning from one metanarrative to another, resolving major conflict in my life. My Life Map testifies to a change from a "contamination script" to a "redemption story" which I now embrace with energy. Just as God brought the miracle of healing into Joseph's family, so I have been able to process personal trauma--the topic of the sixth step in this project, which I have titled "Redeeming the Darkside of my Life." In one of life's great twists and turns, I now bear witness to a truth originally stated by Horace: "Change the name and the story is about you."

SIX

Redeeming the Darkside of my Life:
A Sixth Step in Life Mapping

On the morning of August 7th, 1971, I was scheduled to take a helicopter out of the jungles of Vietnam and board a jet for Sidney, Australia. I had left my one-week R&R to the end of my combat tour with the First Air Cav Division. My "short-timer's calendar" was down to about 14 days yet to be crossed-off. On August 6th it was my turn to run patrol as one of two Radio Telephone Operators in our Army platoon-- Alpha Company, First Battalion of the Seventh Cavalry. Nixon had been elected President on his promise to extract us from this unpopular war. What that meant for us on the battlefield was more dangerous missions with half the personnel.

I casually walked up to the other RTO and he immediately blurted out, "No way, I'm NOT takin' your patrol!" Our 12-man force encountered many live booby traps that morning, then a deadly fire fight with Vietcong insurgents guarding their cache of weapons for a final assault on Saigon. After lifting out four wounded soldiers (one KIA), I stepped on a trip-wired booby trap, a scene I have created here with my PowerPoint vignette. My first reaction after the explosion was "That's it, I'm dead." Then the next thought: "If I'm thinking this, I'm still alive!" I went down, both legs riddled with shrapnel. Time slowed way down, a carousel of my loved ones passing me by as if in a vision … Mom, Dad, brothers Burt, Tom, Dave, Grandpa Eberle, Grandma Sherry, etc. Buddies grabbed my radio and called in the circling medivac chopper to lift out four more men wounded-in-action. This event punctuated the darkest Chapter in my life. I offer it as help toward a sixth step in the Life Map project, "Redeeming the Darkside of my Life."

The American Psychiatric Association defines Posttraumatic Stress Disorder (PTSD) as "a psychiatric disorder that may occur in people who have experienced or witnessed a traumatic event such as a natural disaster, a serious accident, a terrorist act, war/combat, or rape or who have been threatened with death, sexual violence or serious injury." My year of combat in Vietnam left me hypersensitive to sudden noises of any kind. Fireworks make me edgy to this day. In my postwar years, my dreams constantly put be back in combat, my new bride mistaken for an enemy combatant on several occasions. My radioed-in artillery and bomb strikes certainly ended the lives of human beings. Survivor guilt ate away at me, too, as I wondered why good buddies died and I did not. Like most Vietnam veterans, I just tried to forget or bury my story!

PTSD is not the only kind of "darkside" event I have experienced. There was that boy who pulled the chair out from under me as I sat down to my first Cub Scout meeting, sending me out the door and turning me into a "runner" every time life got tough. There was the Christian cult (called Moral Re-Armament) my parents and relatives were pushing as I was trying to figure out my own identity. There was that Hippy phase I experimented with as a young adult that could have left me in a vegetative state! And there was that midlife church conflict (and split) I opened this series with, which got me started on my Life Map project. I think any adult could offer a collection of experiences like mine that have complicated the plot in their story and pushed them up against the proverbial wall. These do factor in on anxiety over Life Mapping. Interestingly, after surveying 100 practitioners of Life Review (a form of Life Mapping), Narrative Psychologist B. J. Haight reported that only seven percent experienced negative reactions. I was in this minority when a church crisis opened me up to this method for navigating difficult challenges in my life.

Then there are those negative events so high on the trauma scale that most of us will deny them in some slim hope that they will just "disappear." The APA definition above surfaced most in this category of darkside events. While some of the negatives in our lives are brought on *by* our own immaturity, foolishness, or sin, these tragically happen *to* us through no fault of our own. Often, they generate thorny philosophical questions like why did this happen to me and where was God (or a parent) when I needed protection? Of the hundred plus adults I shepherded through Life Map creation, about 20% have been subjected to darkside events like sexual violence or spousal abuse. Many of them found the resources of their faith and church sufficient to process the trauma and include it redemptively in their Life Map. Often it was one of their two mentors-- chosen to accompany them in their educational journey--who helped them process and integrate their darkest Chapter with the rest of their life story.

Some of my Bethel Seminary of the East or New England Christian Study Center adults could not get beyond their darkside trauma, even with the help of a pastoral mentor. Several privately requested that their traumatic event be left out of the assignment, while a few others consulted with a counselor for inclusion of the event in their final Life Map presentation. Reflecting now, I should have recommended a professional counselor to several of my students struggling through this step. It is probable that some of them just made a strategic decision to leave this exceedingly difficult part of their life out of public view. But I have my doubts about this, because those who did do the hard work of processing the darkside did present authentic Life Maps that had a huge impact on their family members and mentors, on our class group, and then on the circle of people who witnessed these presentations. I witnessed bonds being formed, forgiveness being experienced, and new mission and purpose emerging. I became convinced, we *can* redeem the darkside of our lives, no matter how traumatic!

In addition, embracing the Biblical Master Story can point the way out of the philosophical dilemma. Christian Apologists Peter Kreeft and Ron Tacelli state this clearly: "Free will is part of our essence. There can be no human being without it. The alternative to free will is not being human but an animal or machine." Tragically, it is the abuse of a good gift of God--this freedom of will--that often is responsible for the evil sting in these darkside experiences. Hardest of all is when that abuse comes at the hand of a relative or close family member!

So why not just leave a difficult event out of my Life Map presentation? This seems to be a reasonable proposal until we stop to consider the conclusions of Narrative Psychologists. Their verdict has been unanimous: Repressed memories from war or any other traumatic experience in life will be a sure roadblock to honest Life Review. In the words of Peter Coleman:

> Assimilation of traumatic experience is necessary for the creation of a satisfactory life story. Without it the story will remain incomplete, its central messages vulnerable to ambiguity and fragmentation.

An additional Coleman criterion for a "successful" Life Review--truth, or simply telling my story honestly from my own perspective--adds weight to this verdict. Here, too, the Christian metanarrative can make a profound difference because it offers me a total reinterpretation of my life retrospectively, integrating past traumatic events in with my story so that my Life Map becomes continuous, intelligible, and coherent. Interestingly, it is the choice of some metanarrative story that counters the fragmentation that many modern autobiographies suffer from.

Spiritual leaders Sam Rima and Gary McIntosh expand the notion of the darkside beyond traumatic events to include the inner urges, compulsions, and dysfunctions of our personalities "that often go unexamined or remain unknown to us until we experience an emotional explosion ... or some other significant problem that causes us to search for the reason why." They outline steps remarkably like Life Mapping for redeeming this darkside--transforming it into a force for good. Practicing "progressive self-knowledge," they urge, can change it into godly ambition for future hope or God's kingdom purposes.

Best practices for redeeming the darkside must begin with an accountability check. Some Life Mappers are going to need a professional counselor to complete this step, or at least a trusted mentor or spiritual director. For me, being wounded in action in Vietnam was the "nadir" or low point of my life--but as Rima and McIntosh suggest, it was my underlying moral and spiritual dysfunction that made me feel like my life was circling into a black hole. Receiving God's offer of forgiveness in Christ was a huge turnaround, but I needed wise counsel to help me process several difficult Chapters in my life, including my war PTSD. If this is the case with you, it is a huge first step to seek help on redeeming the darksde.

The first thing a wise counselor might need to do is help the victim of a serious crime or offense to discern the difference between forgiveness and reconciliation. Forgiving such an offense before God is an act that can bring personal freedom, but reconciliation with the offender (dead or alive) does NOT follow from any Biblical notion of forgiveness. The power in divine forgiveness rests on the huge debt Jesus paid for with His life, as foretold in the parable of the unforgiving servant (Matthew 18:21-35).

The following practices for redeeming the darkside can be completed using a personal journal, accompanied by prayer, feedback from a mentor, or the guidance of a professional counselor:

- *Read, pray, and reflect on how a Biblical person redeemed his or her darkside*, looking up one of the following people using the suggested weblink: Jacob, Joseph, Ruth, Esther, Peter, Paul, or Mary Magdalene. Write about any insights you found to be helpful from your Bible reading (www.biblewise.com/bible_study/characters/)...
- *Describe your darkside experience or event*, being as honest as you can be. Give it a name or title and try to frame this journal entry in the third person singular, "he, she, or it..." Counselors have found that this can be more empowering than when such an event is framed as first person singular. Include your feelings, thoughts, and any specific reactions you now recall.
- *Put this event in a broader context*, reviewing the Chapter of your life in which that darkside event (or state of mind) happened. Who were the key people in your life during this Chapter and what role did they play? Did you share that difficult experience or event with a confidante at the time? What was your spiritual and emotional life like and how was God present to you?
- *Engage in a personal dialog* over this event or trauma, writing out an imaginary dialog with the person or event associated with the darkside. This has the potential for bringing you to a new understanding. In the words of Richard Peace, author of *Spiritual Journaling*: "This is not a mysterious process. We know from experience that in conversation we work out our questions, we sort through our ideas until they are clear, and we realize things that we had not been aware of ... Imagination can be a powerful tool for growth." What feelings are evoked? What new things can you learn about this event or relationship? Share this journal entry with a person of trust, discussing what it means to "redeem" this? How might you include this in your Life Map?

Ironically, the lowest point in my life (my *nadir*) led directly to my highest point (or zenith). As I look back from the vantage point of faith, I now see that being wounded in Vietnam not only gave me a vision of my loved ones, but it triggered a crisis of faith that led to forgiveness and a "new leaf." In just two years--a Chapter in my Life Map I titled "Caught by the Draft" (December 1969 to Dec. 1971)--I nearly lost my leg, spent months in an Army hospital, found God, met my wife-to-be Ingelise, and discovered my life's purpose and mission. One of the teachable moments in that chain of events happened as I lay in bed one night. Now faced with physical disability, years of spiritual and moral bankruptcy came pressing in on me, and I voiced what I now recognize as the skeptic's prayer: "God, I don't even know your name, but if You are listening, I am ready to turn to you for help." That was my hinge, my crucial turning-point!

In the language of Narrative Psychology, my life had been following a painful "contamination script" of boredom, passivity, and victimhood. The next day I met a couple who invited me to receive Jesus as Lord and Savior. It was as if a light went on in my darkened soul. My life has now morphed into a "redemption story," yet with difficult challenges, but full of hope, love, and purpose. The practices outlined in this chapter are aimed at helping the Life Mapper follow a similar trajectory. Redeeming the darkside has the potential for recasting it as positive or at least taking the sting out of it. The next or seventh step will be the search for an image or metaphor which "crowns" or unifies my life story.

SEVEN

Is There an Image that "Crowns" My Life Story? My Seventh Step in Life Mapping

On December 23rd, 1971, I received a phone call from the pastor of Ridgeway Alliance Church extending me this invitation: "Noel, I heard you prayed to receive Jesus as your Savior last night, congratulations! Would you be willing to come to our Christmas eve service tomorrow and share your testimony?" Dahl Sekenger was the pastor of my parent's home church in White Plains, NY, and I think he was a bit taken aback by the long pause on my end of the phone. I had indeed invited Jesus to be my Lord and Savior at a Christmas Party hosted by several families in his church. Something important had happened to me! I had reached a real low point after stepping on a booby trap grenade in Vietnam in August. Just a day before this party I had cried out to God asking for His help with my messed-up life. That help came fast and I was still trying to process these momentous events. Now I was recipient of this strange invitation.

The first thing that went through my head was, "I am NOT a public speaker." The slide I created to memorialize this event records my delayed response: "Hello Pastor, yes I did, but what do you mean by a 'testimony.' Have I done something wrong?" "No," he laughed, "I mean, what happened with you last night, just tell your story." Despite inner reservations, I did not feel I could say no to my parent's Pastor. And so it was that this word "testimony" which has multiple meanings, became the metaphor I picked because it best unifies all the chapters in my life story. This next step in the seventh chapter for the participant in this project is a guide to choosing an image or metaphor that brings unity to the Chapters in your Life Map.

MY TESTIMONY

December 24, 1971

Pastor Dahl Seckinger: "Noel, I heard you prayed to receive Jesus as your Savior... Would you come to our Christmas eve service and share your testimony?

Noel: "Hello Pastor, Yes I did, but what do you mean by a "testimony?"

Ridgeway Alliance Church - White Plains, New York

Yes, I did blurt out this question to the pastor, "have I done something wrong?" The first thing that popped into my head when I heard this word was "a solemn declaration made by a witness under oath in response to court interrogation," its primary and popular meaning (Merriam-Webster). His laughter tipped me off to the special meaning which I soon came to cherish--testimony as "a public profession of religious experience." God's answer to this skeptic's prayer was quick indeed, but it also became my major turning-point, marking off a "before" and an "after" for my life story. My Life Map project got me to reflect on my past with brand new eyes, in fresh awareness that God had been present from the beginning, often through mentors who cared about me as a person created in God's image. In time, "testimony" rose to a crowning position, a metaphor unifying all the Chapters in my life and thus an apt title for my Life Map project.

For the hundred plus adults I have had the privilege of mentoring through their Life Map projects, an image or metaphor often emerged suddenly as they journaled through their life Chapters from birth to present. Often it came as an aha moment, a flash of insight about how they could organize and share their presentation. This development was always very inspiring because writing out 20+ pages in a journal with the details on each of their life-Chapters became a bit of a drag, week after week. This creative breakthrough excited them to complete the project and share the results with the group of adults they had come to trust and appreciate. I as group facilitator especially enjoyed these discoveries which I had informed them to be on the lookout for.

Often their ideas were sparked by a hobby or interest--sharing their story using a cartoon, poem, painting, or song arrangement composed for each life-Chapter. One adult was an antique collector, pulling out items from an old treasure chest to narrate each of her Chapters. Another, a welder, crafted an iron-rod timeline for explaining his life story. A quilter put in the time to design her timeline in the shape of a nautilus shell, her life-story spiraling from the center-point outward.

Then there were Life Map presentations centered around an activity, such as the student telling his story using food, his wife passing out a food sample connected with each of his Chapters, cheerios for childhood, pizza in his teens, and then a climactic closing--a celebration of the Communion meal. The content of these presentations was of most importance, of course, but the creative media used to communicate the content made for more assured presenters and a rapt audience, lending weight to Marshall McLuhan's trademark proverb, "the medium is the message."

In some cases, an image or metaphor emerged directly from the journaling they were completing for their Life Map Chapters. One man who had been freed from a destructive lifestyle with the help of Alcoholics Anonymous, struggled over how to present his story to his group. He was puzzling over a recent spiritual experience related to the cross of Christ, when it suddenly dawned on him: His story could be told as a collection of puzzle pieces, the climactic "crucifix piece" completing the picture painted by his metaphor. A female student who had saved significant pieces of clothing as she grew up, hung each item on a clothesline strung across the classroom as she narrated her story. Each piece of clothing displayed a Chapter in her story, with reference to the Apostle Paul's metaphor of being clothed with Christ (Galatians 3:27). A third Life Mapper presented his story via PowerPoint slides, the difficult darkside event in his life depicted by black--a totally darkened slide--symbolic of the trauma he related with some emotion. The group got the point of the metaphor!

One of my favorite spiritual autobiographies is that of Blaise Pascal (1623-1662), who chose a metaphor like mine as the image that brought unity to his life-story. This philosophical and scientific genius had a dramatic spiritual moment in 1654, which he wrote down and then sewed right into the lining of his coat, discovered after his death at age 39. Here is the substance of what he titled his "Memorial:"

> In the year of Grace, 1654. On Monday, 23rd of November ... from about half past ten in the evening until about half past twelve. Fire. God of Abraham, God of Isaac, God of Jacob, not of the philosophers and scholars (Ex. 3:6, Matt. 22:32). Certitude. Feeling. Joy. Peace. God of Jesus Christ ... Greatness of the human soul (John 17:25). Joy, joy, joy, tears of joy ... I have separated myself from Him: I have fled from Him, denied Him, crucified Him ... We keep hold of Him only by the ways taught in the Gospel. Renunciation, total and sweet. Total submission to Jesus Christ and to my director (Psalm 119:16). Amen

Pascal transferred his hand-written Memorial from one piece of clothing to the next until the end of his days, a reminder of Jesus' gracious acceptance despite his persistent denials. This was very personal for Pascal, and I think of my Life Map's metaphor in a very similar light. From its strict legal meaning, Testimony evolved its specialized usage for a person's religious life, and in that sense became the "metaphor of choice" for my entire spiritual journey.

James Dillon--a Psychology professor since 1974--has facilitated spiritual life writing with hundreds of students at the State University of West Georgia. Dillon observed that adults in his spiritual autobiography groups discovered the "inner continuity" that ran through their lives through resonant images. His comments are highly relevant to this seventh step in the Life Map project:

> These images are dynamic and typically very simple--a blooming flower, a shooting ray of sunlight, the peeling of an onion, wandering in a desert, floating down a river,

building a house, climbing a staircase or a mountain--but they are powerful and meaningful for both author and reader alike.

Interestingly, he found that 82 percent of his students agreed that writing their story from a spiritual perspective "put them in touch with a dynamic and resonant force behind and within their lives that helped give their lives new meaning, coherence, and direction." That was my discovery, too!

There is a solid research basis for this seventh step in the Life Map project. While not all adults in my Introduction to Spiritual Formation classes found an image or metaphor for their Life Map, Greenberg and Knowlton found that for both visualizers and verbalizers, visual imagery was associated with the sense that the presenter was actually reliving their memories. Their conclusion from three experiments with autobiographical memory was this: "The results support the idea that visual imagery plays a vital and irreplaceable role in autobiographical recall." Dillon found three themes around which his students organized their autobiographies, (1) as a response to a key question (39%), by casting life in relation to an important event or person, sometimes a trauma (34%), or by seeing one's life in lost-and-found terms (20%). My Life Map best fits that latter category.

As for an assignment for this seventh step--selecting an image or metaphor for my story-- a journal entry is not necessary, but a decision or two need to be made as you prepare to share your final presentation. Is there a hobby or activity you can plan to use for creatively sharing your Life Map? How could that organize each of your life-Chapters? And has an image or metaphor emerged from your journaling reflections that will help you finalize an outline for your presentation and communicate what is most important to you? This part of the project piggybacks on the third step in which an outline gets carved out of hinge events that bookended my life-Chapters.

The Testimony metaphor did not come to me until after I had first presented my Life Map to my classes. An early decision I made with my Life Map project was to prepare it as a PowerPoint presentation, an easy way to share it with groups. Being an amateur artist, I stumbled on the idea of drawing up teachable moments from my life using my "PowerPoint vignettes," partly because I possessed no photos of these important events. I thus created one vignette for each of my Chapters. Later as I reflected on my storyline (the fourth step), it dawned on me that my first public Testimony perfectly captured the resolution of the conflict in my life's plot. This word that tripped me up in 1971 with its funny double meaning, nailed down my decision on an image or metaphor: Testimony it would be.

Standing up in front of my parent's congregation on that Christmas eve was my first public Testimony, and it was short and sweet. I recall mispronouncing the book of Job as a job one gets paid for--one clue about the life crisis I had just come through. Yet that event became a highpoint in my life in more ways than one--first as a metaphor that served as the interpretive key to my past, present, and future, and then as the moment when I met my wife-to-be, Ingelise Mogensen, a Danish *Au Pair* residing with another church family. I have now integrated details and pictures from her story into my Life Map. My Testimony is so important to me now that I would like to sew a summary of it into my coat the way Pascal did with his Memorial. While I probably will not do that, I have come to treasure the opportunities I have had to share my Life Map Testimony with family and friends. Which is the next or eighth step in this project, "Sharing My Life Story in a Supportive Group."

EIGHT

Sharing My Life Story in a Supportive Group: Eighth Step in Life Mapping

I vividly remember the feelings of fear and insecurity I had to overcome to stand up and present my story in front of a group of people. As Director of the New England Center of Bethel Seminary of the East, I was assigned to teach the introductory course for new adult students. A major teaching objective for that course was this Life Map project. The most frequent questions I received from my students were these: "What is a Life Map?" and "Do I have to present mine?" The best answer to both questions was my sharing mine with the class. This chapter on "Sharing My Life Story in a Supportive Group" is thus written as a guide for this important public step in the Life Map project, one often accompanied by "stage fright" or hesitancy about opening my life to others. Three roles will be looked at for this "grand finale," the leader's role in organizing the sharing session, the group member's role in sharing his or her Life Map, and some suggestions for the rest of the group as each Life Map is presented.

Here in my PowerPoint vignette, Bethel student Mary Sue Strautin presents her Life Map using an item of clothing that she had saved from each Chapter of her life, including a sweater her mom knitted for her before she died, a Liberty University graduation gown and stole, wedding dress, and T-shirts from her mission work in Swaziland and home state of Wisconsin. As she shared each chapter, she hung the piece of clothing up on the line tied across the classroom, ending with a summary that went something like this: "And there is my life in all of its colors, shapes, and texture … God 'hems' us in, lays His hand upon us, and completes us." Mary Sue adopted this powerful sewing metaphor from Psalm 139, verse 5, as the unifying image for her life. This communicated her story very powerfully.

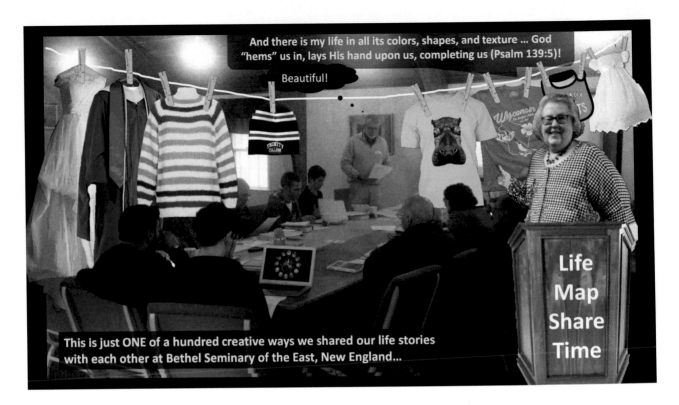

This is just ONE of a hundred creative ways we shared our life stories with each other at Bethel Seminary of the East, New England…

Group Leader's Role in Structuring the Life Map Sharing

It is assumed that the leader of a Life Map small group has first gone through the process of creating a Life Map, because his or her sharing that project will set the tone for the group. It will answer basic questions such as what a Life Map is, how to go about preparing one, how much time to take in presenting it, and what the key take-aways should be. In my experience as a leader, thirty to forty-five minutes is a good rule-of-thumb for each presentation. I used timecards of "10, 5, and one-minute" (remaining), which I displayed as a means of time management. Richard Peace in his *Spiritual Autobiography* states why this is so important (p. 51):

> Who can compress an entire life into thirty minutes? The presenter's challenge is
> to select the key issues, incidents, and insights to share and to set aside others.
> The hardest thing is to decide what to leave out of your story.

In a three-hour session, three people can thus share. For a ten-person group, that would mean a final three sessions dedicated to sharing Life Maps. Another option would be to set aside a Saturday in a retreat format for the group's presentations, lunching together at the midpoint. The following offers a four-part schedule for a Life Map sharing session:

Opening a Sharing Session (2 minutes)

The small group leader initiates the sharing session by spending a few minutes in prayer, asking for God's guidance, a relaxed and enjoyable presentation, clarity for the presenter, good insights in the follow-up discussion, and a closing time of affirmation.

The Life Map Presentation (45 minutes)

While this series of chapters could be used as a guide to complete a Life Map by an individual, the benefits of doing this project with a group make that second option preferable. There are the barriers that often surface during the project timeframe that need to be overcome, such as the discipline of journaling, the time required to reflect on our life's story, hesitancy about opening up to a new group of people, and a willingness to work through a difficult experience. The leader and members of a supportive group take on the role of cheerleaders to encourage each person through barriers like this to get to the finish line.

Presenting my life story with a group can be another significant barrier, especially for adults who see themselves as introverts. The trust-building and interest in each other's story that grows through several months of meeting together go a long way to overcoming this barrier. Each Life Map presentation will be so unique and moving, that as soon as the sharing of presentations has begun, other group members will anticipate the many positives that accompany this "grand finale." In my experience with Bethel Seminary of the East and New England Christian Study Center students, this Life Map sharing was not only a highlight for the course, but of the whole educational experience. Often mentors, spouses, pastors, and friends were invited to witness Life Map presentations, making it transformative for a wider circle of people. Richard Peace highlights this for us well (p. 49):

> Writing a spiritual autobiography usually brings great insight … But it is even better to share our spiritual autobiography with others. It is as if in making our private musings public we accept who we are in a new way. Private and public selves merge into a healthy unity. Receiving feedback from friends who have heard our spiritual autobiography is affirming and insightful.

The steps in this series of chapters are aimed at helping each presenter be well-prepared, be as honest as the level of group trust allows, be respectful of the time considerations outlined by the leader, and be open to group feedback after the presentation has ended.

Feedback & Discussion (10 minutes)

The audience for each presentation has an important supportive role as well. The following are suggestions: To listen in an empathetic way, to give the presenter full attention, to not interpret, correct, or criticize, and to have the following questions in mind in preparation for a brief time of feedback and discussion:

- What is similar or different from your own story? What is striking to you?
- What do you learn from the story, what insights are there for you?
- What if anything puzzles you in this story? What would you like to understand better?
- What special gifts do you see in the presenter, what is unique about his or her story?
- Are there any implications here for the presenter's purpose, mission, or future?

A participation sheet prepared by the small group leader for members to use could be a helpful exercise as they witness each presentation. Peace adds this helpful suggestion (p. 52):

When the presentation is finished, begin the discussion by going around the circle and asking each person to identify, very briefly, one element of the presentation he or she most appreciated. Continue this spirit of affirmation throughout the discussion.

A Prayer of Blessing (3 minutes)

A practice I found meaningful in my seminary and study center groups was holding hands in a circle with the presenter and inviting members to ask God to bless and empower the presenter going forward. This might or might not be a good idea post Covid-19. The group leader should close each sharing session with affirmation for the presenter and thanks to God for the presentation. These sessions have always been memorable, particularly when the presenter has invited guests to be present.

I will never forget Mary Sue Strautin's Life Map presentation. For one thing, she only used 30 of the 45 minutes of time allotted to her, which was unusual. Her clothing collection perfectly communicated a key experience from each Chapter of her life. A connecting "thread," the clothing metaphor provided by Psalm 139:5 and Ephesians 4:24, knit her life-story together simply and powerfully. Then her husband Imants was thrilled to be part of the whole learning experience, after he had strung the clothesline across the classroom for her to hang her laundry on. Class members were curious about their years of missionary service in Swaziland, asking question after question! For me as teacher it was truly one of those magical moments in the classroom. We ended by holding hands and blessing Mary Sue and Imants in their calling to serve the Lord in music and chaplaincy going forward. That "forward" or future aspect will take up the next (nineth) step in the Life Map project.

NINE

Reflecting My Story into the Future: A Nineth Step in a Life Map Project

Enroute to Vietnam in September of 1970, my itinerary took me from the Oakland Army Base in California through Anchorage, Alaska, to Tokyo and then on to Saigon. It was an emotional trip, getting shuffled into a new group of soldiers on each leg of that trek to fight in an unpopular war. The stop in Anchorage was brief, three to four hours, with a walk outside the airport lounge in full view of the mountains surrounding the site of one of the worst earthquakes of all time. Caught up in the magnitude of that moment, I also recall saying out loud, "I shall return to see these snow-covered mountains again." This was for me almost like a prophesy--words once spoken that would somehow have to come to pass. But echoing in my head were the words of that iconic Vietnam soldier, on whose helmet was scribbled, "War is Hell!" While this PowerPoint vignette from my life could be viewed as a quirky episode linking my past, present, and (hoped for) future, a Life Map will include an important future dimension, which I explore in this nineth step for this project.

33

The best illustration of this comes from Saint Augustine's *Confessions*, written in Latin and completed in 397 AD. This seminal work is not only the first in this brand-new genre of literature, but it became "the Augustinian formula" for all future self-writing -- (Life Mapping being a contemporary form of this kind of writing). Written in three parts, Augustine's spiritual autobiography began with "confession" as penitence, but its title morphed in meaning to self-awareness in part-two and then to faith in an all-knowing God as Augustine focused on the future. Part-one concludes with Augustine as the unconverted protagonist crying out in exasperation, "I have become an enigma to myself" (4.4.9). Augustine's role shifts to that of the enlightened narrator in part-two, now marking the turning-point of his life: "Lord, you set me down before my face, forcing me to mark how despicable I was" (8.7.16). After his conversion, part-three then unveils Augustine's ultimate quest for union with God, with the following deeper insights expressed about his future hope and expectation (11.20.26):

> You [Lord] are the king of your creation; tell me, then: how do you instruct people's minds about the future? You did so teach the prophets ... It might properly be said, "There are three tenses or times: the present of past things, the present of present things, and the present of future things." These are three realities in the mind, but nowhere else as far as I can see, for the present of past things is memory, the present of present things is attention, and the present of future things is expectation.

My Life Map follows the Augustinian formula closely, with my turning-point conversion also occurring when I was a young adult, prompting me to reinterpret my past experiences, my present identity, and my mission going forward. The dramatic plot shift in my story helped me to gain a sense of calling to pastor and teach, a very different vocation from what I had pursed up to that point. I soon discovered that the divine Potter had been guiding my life-journey from the beginning, with distinct moments of epiphany which I have captured in my vignettes and used in this series on constructing a Life Map.

Interestingly, the church crisis that introduced me to this ancient practice of spiritual autobiography or Life Mapping posed a sharp challenge to my sense of mission or calling to serve the Lord as a pastor-teacher. That conflict put my future in jeopardy! My Life Map project reconnected me to the "Big Story" of Scripture and to the Lord who had repurposed my life. Augustine's union with God was my hope, too.

One practitioner adopted a new word to refer to this future aspect of spiritual autobiography. A Life Map project will help a person to reflect on the past with new eyes and it will invite him or her to "proflect" on the future as well. David Alberts defined "proflection" as "considering possible future trajectories based upon past experience." The adult students I had the privilege of mentoring on their Life Map projects at Bethel Seminary of the East and the New England Christian Study Center expressed this future sense in a wide variety of ways, as a *calling*, a *mission* to engage in, their *purpose* in service and ministry, and even as a *destiny* that their faith invited them into. Sometimes it was a mentor who pointed them in this future direction, often reinforced by the group after their final presentation.

For one student this project helped him bring closure to a painful leadership conflict and reaffirm a *calling* to plant and pastor new churches. The project helped another student and her spouse write a *mission* statement, with fresh motivation to take the first steps to implement that mission immediately. Another couple involved in lay leadership in their church noticed during their project journaling that God had used them to strengthen several marriages, with a decision that this would become their shared ministry *purpose* going forward. Several Life Mappers even adopted the word *destiny* to describe God's hidden "Hand" guiding them into the work they were born to accomplish. Each of these words point towards a future "based upon past experience."

There is yet another way the Life Map project can assist us when it comes to the future. Not all transitions--or "hinge events" between the Chapters in our lives--involve smooth sailing. One of my most recent hinge events happened in 2013 when Minnesota's Bethel University made the difficult financial decision to close its East Coast centers. In a late Friday afternoon phone call, their New England director was face-to-face with the end of a life-Chapter, one I had hoped would take me up to retirement. It was a job I loved and one that fulfilled my calling as pastor-teacher! I had brought our 40 Bethel Seminary of the East adults through the admissions process and now I had to break this news to them in the middle of a semester. It was one of the most difficult things I have had to do. At 65 years of age, my wife Ingelise and I agonized over what the next Chapter in our lives would look like.

After about a month of grieving over this unwelcome ending which I referred to as "Getting the Axe," I decided to pick up where my Life Map project had left off. Ingelise and I walked together through the steps outlined in this series of chapters, with spiritual journaling, prayer, and counsel from several mentors pointing us back to the Big Story of the Bible and to our Lord who had guided us through past transitions and life Chapters. Several positive tasks emerged around a new Chapter which I titled "I Must be a Lifelong Learner," including working on a Doctor in Ministry degree, research on our family trees, and the launching of a new school for training church leaders which we named the New England Christian Study Center.

Our sails soon filled up again with faith and hope, Ingelise taking the lead on ministry to our growing family circle! This new Chapter has been summative and integrative for us as older adults, adding a thirteenth to our growing Life Map project. Anticipating future transitions and Chapters can be formative for a young adult and restorative for a person weathering a midlife crisis. Many of my students included the expectation of future transitions and Chapters as part of their Life Map projects.

The following exercises will help the Life Mapper to "proflect" with the future in view. Set aside several journaling sessions in the coming week to respond to the following three queries which are borrowed from Dan McAdam's "Life Story Interview" questions:

- First, please describe **a positive future**. That is, please describe what you would like to happen in the future for your life story, including what goals and dreams you might accomplish or realize in the future. Please try to be realistic in doing this. In other words, I would like you to give me a picture of what you would realistically like to see happen in the future chapters and scenes of your life story.
- Now, please describe **a negative future**. That is, please describe a highly undesirable future for yourself, one that you fear could happen to you that you hope does not happen. Again, try to be pretty realistic. In other words, I would like you to give me a picture of a negative future fo your life story that could possibly happen but that you hope will not happen.

- Looking back over your entire life story as a story with chapters and scenes, extending into the past as well as an imagined future, can you discern **a central theme, message, or idea** that runs throughout your story? What is the major theme of your life story? Explain…

For extra credit, reflect on what you have written in your journal for these three questions and then try put into words (30 or less) **a life mission statement** that would serve you going forward.

My return to Alaska in the fall of 2018 was not only the fulfillment of a whispered prophesy after surviving a war, but now I was sharing it with my best friend and spouse, Ingelise, after fifty years of life together. It is hard to describe my feelings on that milestone trip. Witnessing snow-covered Denali, the tallest mountain in the western hemisphere, was deeply moving for both of us, albeit for different reasons. Both of us were impressed with the vastness and wildness of this frontier State. My Life Map reflects the Augustinian formula in yet another way, with its distinct Biblical plot line, beginning with creation, descending in a Fall, but then unexpectedly rising with an act of redemption. My Anchorage vignette points to a future of hope and expectation, which leads to the last or tenth step in a Life Map project: What is the legacy I want to pass on to my circle of friends and family?

TEN

Passing On a Legacy: A Tenth Step in the Life Mapping Project

When I reflect on my family legacy, I immediately think of a father and son campout my dad described in a book he penned late in life to record his one-liners and life-lessons gleaned in raising four boys on a salesman's salary. That trek took us into the wilderness of the Adirondack Mountains in upstate, NY, a hike he said his sons "took him on."

I say "took me" advisedly because of various outings and overnights … at this time there was no question who took who. They planned everything to the smallest detail. In fact, I didn't even know what we were going to eat until they took the cans out of their packs.

My vignette shows my dad enjoying his favorite pastime while my brothers Tom and Dave join me at the campfire we built by the stream where we set up four shelters for sleeping. A book on Campcraft inspired us to build natural shelters of stick, bark, moss, and pine boughs, lean-to's that would keep out the weather and the wildlife. All the camping details on this trip were left up to us kids per our request. With his typical humor, Dad observed, "The boys had blown their predator-calling whistle so we could expect a half-grown wildcat at least! The only sounds were the gurgling of the little waterfall nearby and the soughing of the breezes in the pine trees." It was an unforgettable time of bonding that stands out as I think of the legacy that my family-of-origin bequeathed to me. This tenth chapter explores that notion of "Passing on a Legacy," utilizing a Life Map project as an important part of that task.

A Father & Son Campout

3.5 Miles North of Twitchell Lake, on the Other Side of Razorback Pond

My parents' legacy to us boys included the gift of a log cabin on Twitchell Lake in Big Moose, NY, 3.5 miles from where we launched this unforgettable hike in the summer of 1961. Defining the noun "legacy" begins with "a gift by will, especially of money or other personal property" (Merriam-Webster). But then this word expands into its second meaning, more intangible (and important) than the first—which encompasses all that my parents transmitted to us boys by way of genes, character, and accomplishments. From them I received my loyalty to my wife, my passion for art and writing, my love for nature and the wilderness, my commitment to learning, my community activism, and my love for people who are different from me racially and ethnically. The faith in God Dad and Mom embraced later in life has become a crowning part of my legacy, taking a central place in my vocation and calling.

Interestingly, a third meaning of the word legacy is also illustrated by my Adirondack vignette. My father Norm helped to found an association called Sunset Parking, which gave his sons membership in an organization that provides parking for cars and storage for the boat we need to reach that log cabin located on a remote shore of the highest inhabited lake of these mountains.

So, what does this have to do with Life Mapping? Simply, my Life Map is an eloquent expression of the legacy my wife Ingelise and I hope to pass on to our children and grandchildren, with a focus on the second and more important meaning for this word. My project is in presentation format, using PowerPoint media with a brief explanation for each slide. As soon as I write out a detailed narrative for my Life Map project, that work will become my memoirs (plural), my spiritual autobiography. My Dad's book *Discover Your Miracle* was his memoirs and ultimately a testimony to his faith in God. Richard Peace makes this point in his workbook on *Spiritual Autobiography*:

> This is one reason why it is so useful to write a spiritual autobiography. It draws
> the strands of our lives together in a way that points to their meaning; it reminds

us of where true reality lies in contrast to the illusions of modern life. A spiritual autobiography encourages us to notice God, and as we notice, our lives are changed.

Marysue Strautin, graduate of Bethel Seminary of the East and now retired hospice chaplain, recorded and transcribed the life stories of senior adults and invited the whole family to be present for the reading. She noted the power of intergenerational bonding in these events, with themes of gratitude, forgiveness, and legacy celebrated. The ministry potential here is immense and untapped. My suggestion for this tenth chapter is to pass on my Life Map to my circle of family and friends as the main expression of my life and my legacy. Technology offers us many venues for this, including a narrated PowerPoint, a video recording, or typed-up spiritual memoirs. My recorded Life Map will be a central part of what I bequeath to my children and grandchildren.

The following counsel is offered for taking a Life Map and turning it into spiritual memoirs:

- A first step would be simply to **write out a narrative for my Life Map**, answering each of the questions which were posed for the third chapter in this series titled "The Hinge Events that Moved Me in New Directions." That step in my Life Map project generated an outline for my Life Map, with Chapter titles and dates. Essentially this would come word-for-word from the journal you kept for this project. This typed-up journal then becomes your spiritual memoirs (in draft).
- Several of the steps in this series of chapters could **add important elements to my memoir**, such as teachable moments (step 2), my life's storyline (4), how I relate to a Master story (5), redeeming my darkside (6), and a metaphor that unifies my life story (7). Any of the material I have written for these in my journal could be added to my narrative script at an appropriate point. These might be addressed as part of an introduction or a conclusion.
- **Editing and polishing** would be a next writing task for the memoirs, should I have an interest in trying to publish it. A member of my family circle might be glad to do this for me if he or she has editing experience. Some publishing companies specialize in spiritual memoirs.

Elizabeth Jarrett Andrew has written extensively on the topic of spiritual memoirs, with a listing of 10 "classic" examples that include Augustine and Teresa of Avila, along with 83 contemporary ones--including Rachel Carson and Marjery Kempe. With many of her examples outside the Judeo-Christian tradition, they all share three key qualities: (a) uncovering what is sacred in a life-story; (b) putting a story in a broader sacred context; and (c) telling a story in such a way that it is understandable to the reader. For Andrew, writing out a spiritual autobiography becomes an avenue for prayer and a means of spiritual growth. She summarizes the effort to revise and polish my life story in written form this way:

A well-crafted work welcomes readers in, takes their hats and coats, and gives a thorough tour of the house. The readers then feel enough at ease to dwell in the story for a while, and perhaps be changed by it.

There is one more avenue I included in my project. My Life Map adds a slide titled "My Family Tree" which grew out of research into family genealogy and journaling based on *A Family Genogram Workbook*. The latter resource helped me uncover important emotional relationship patterns in my "family system." It turns out there are amazingly positive "redemption stories" on the Sherry, Eberle, Hayes, and Dumas branches of my Tree, which my adult children and grandkids have been inspired by. There are also some negative examples to learn from, with discovery of a few lurking "skeletons in the closet."

One of the highlights of my parenting has been the campouts and hikes I have taken my children on into the Adirondack wilderness, inspired no doubt by that 1961 "Father & Son Campout." Those occasions have provided some of my best opportunities to share stories from my Life Map legacy. Identifying wildflowers, catching trout from a stream, and naming the tallest trees on the trail--my love for nature and the wilderness is being passed on. Most tellingly, my father's memoir and my Life Map have borne witness to a faith in God we both embraced later in life. I still remember my brothers Tom and Dave bracing my father's hands on either side as Dad jumped across a small stream on our return trip. He ended his account of that memorable campout with this:

> I had survived my ordeal and could now consider myself a full-fledged member of their hiking fraternity. Perhaps the giant leap over that stream had helped to bridge the Generation Gap!

An Update with Helps for the Leader of a Life Map Group

I sit by the fire in our log cabin on Twitchell Lake in Big Moose, NY, and reflect on 72 years of life with my best friend and spouse, Ingelise. We have survived the worst pandemic in 100 years, Covid-19, and prepare to have our three adult children and nine grandchildren join us for another summer in the wilderness. My Life Map has grown to fourteen chapters, the latest titled "We Are Senior's Now." This began with a surprise 70th birthday celebration pulled off by Katrina, Peter, and Luke, our three, with a surprise appearance from Noel's brother Burt and Ingelise's brother Finn from Denmark. Special trips to the Grand Canyon, Bornholm, and Alaska have taken us back to our roots and forward to visit a few special places in our spiritual journey. Sharing those with each other was amazing! Each Chapter of my Life Map is accompanied by a piece of music that was meaningful to me at the time. That was a creative angle which came to me as I journaled my way through my Life Chapters.

Our mission now consists of mentoring our grandkids and inviting our Journey Church adults in Worcester, MA, to join in on its Growth Groups--including one on Life Mapping. I continue to enjoy the research and writing I began in the last Chapter of my life when I completed a Doctor in Ministry degree program with Bethel Seminary. With Ingelise I offer up a prayer that in life we will finish well. And I put a period on this series of chapters aimed at renewing this ancient practice that holds out such promise for spiritual reflection and forward-looking "proflection." My Life Mapping has guided us through three major life-transitions now and our lives have more and more resembled the plot of a hopeful and exciting redemption story!

Helps for the Leader The following Helps are offered to any adult who feels called to host a group like this. Group size should not exceed 8 to 9 adults max, with couples having the option of doing a Life Map together or as individuals. Since Life Map sharing will take about an hour, three adults can share in one meeting, so that a group of 9 will require three meetings for this important climactic activity.

Promotion & Publicity A decision to lead a Life Map group should be made by an adult who has been through the process and is convinced of its value for others. The best publicity is a video testimonial that briefly touches on what a Life Map is with the impact it has had for the leader. Content in these chapters could inform written promotional material. Ten to twelve small group meetings should be planned to allow adults the time to work through these steps to completion and sharing of a Life Map. On a weekly schedule that equals three months, meeting bi-weekly it would encompass about 6 months, with two to three-hour sessions allowing ample time for building trust and sharing progress toward the goal. The invitation to join the group should stress the commitment to weekly journaling with completion and sharing of a Life Map

The First Small Group Session The first session will set the tone and typical agenda for meetings going forward. Each session should begin with a trust-building activity, a search of the internet providing a good collection of these to choose from. The leader can expand on his or her adventure with Life Mapping or spiritual autobiography here, inviting each group member to "circle share" about his or her reason for joining the group and expectations for what will be learned. Sharing something on the light or humorous side, too, can "break the ice," because it is likely that more than one group member may have a concern or fear regarding the Life Map project. A simple group covenant can be offered for members to agree to, with regular attendance, weekly journaling, and a reading of the chapters in this series before each session, included. A point could be included in the covenant regarding privacy--what is shared in the group is confidential; no member will be expected to share anything beyond his or her comfort level. Selection of a mentor or counselor can be touched on for members who indicate they need to process a difficult darkside experience as part of their project--or this could be done privately. Setting up a spiritual journal will be discussed with an assignment to complete at least one journal entry and a reading of the second step, "Inspired by Life's Teachable Moments," in prep for the second session. Each journal entry could focus on one teachable moment in a member's life.

Sessions The second session would be an ideal one for the leader to share his or her Life Map, since that is one of the questions members are likely to come to group with: "What is a Life Map?" Good discussion could follow that in anticipation of the steps for the project. This would also be the perfect time to invite sharing about how the early journaling experiences went. What was easy about it? How did members find it to be challenging and why? Each member should be encouraged to share about one teachable moment in his or her life. Different kinds of teachable moments would make interesting group discussion. Sharing of life's teachable moments will "prime the pump" for Life Mapping, motivating group members to embrace the project. It is likely that group members will also have questions related to the upcoming steps in creating a Life Map, so be prepared to respond to a range of questions.

Sessions 3 through 7 A good agenda for these next five sessions would include trust-building exercises, discussion questions related to the session topic, journaling insights members are willing to share with each other, and a preparation for the upcoming session. Here are some suggested discussion questions for each session, though the leader may want to form his or her own based on a reading of this material:

> *Session 3* "Hinge Events that Moved Me in New Directions"- Share one of the hinge events recorded in your journal that was positive (or negative) for you ... How many Chapters do you come up with using the hinge events as markers? Did some of your hinge events happen "inside" a Chapter? What was it like for you to name (and date) your life Chapters? Can you share a few of your titles? What was it like using Peace's six questions to journal through your most recent Chapter? Note to the Leader: It may be helpful to ask group members to send you a listing of life Chapters with titles and dates, for you to OK them as a Life Map outline. A young adult may have as few as six chapters or less while a senior adult may have up to 12 (or more).

Session 4 "Discovering the Storyline in My Life"- Was there a current event in your lifetime that had a significant impact on you? What was your favorite story as a child and why? Of the story elements listed for the Joseph story, which was of most interest to you? What makes this Biblical story a "metanarrative" or "story of destiny." Journaling through the story elements for your life may have been challenging. Which of these was most revealing or insightful for you? Which was most difficult? How might you show this on your Life Map timeline or in your final presentation?

Session 5 "Connecting My Story in with a Master Story"- Why do you think we as individuals need to have our life stories grounded in a greater reality or metanarrative? Which of the "C" words (Creation, Chaos, Covenant, Christ, Church, & Consummation) that make up God's Big Story do you most relate to and why? How has God's Master Story helped you to make sense of your past, present, and future? How might your life story be different if you had no connection with a metanarrative or bigger story? In what ways can you reflect this connection with a bigger story in your final Life Map presentation?

Session 6 "Redeeming the Darkside of my Life"- Respond to the following quote from my sixth chapter: "I think any adult could offer a collection of experiences like mine that have complicated the plot in their story and pushed them up against the proverbial wall." Briefly, what are some of the events or incidents that have complicated the plot in your life story? Research has shown that there are enormous benefits to processing and integrating the darkest event in your life as an important part of your life story, making it "continuous, intelligible, and coherent." What help do you think you may need to reach this goal? Which of the steps for redeeming your darkside did you find to be most helpful?

Session 7 "Is There an Image that "Crowns" My Life Story?"- Is there a hobby or activity I can plan to use for creatively sharing my Life Map? How could that organize each of my life-Chapters? And has an image or metaphor emerged from my journaling reflections on each of the Chapters on my timeline that will help me finalize an outline for my presentation and communicate what is most important to me? Not everyone has such an image or metaphor but sharing in a group by those who do can often stimulate the creative juices for others to discover one for themselves. How do you see yourself incorporating this in your Life Map intro or conclusions? In each Chapter of your life?

Sessions 8-10 for Sharing Life Maps The leader or facilitator of a Life Map group should have a plan and a schedule that allows each group member approximately an hour to share his or her Life Map (45 minutes max) and receive group feedback (15 minutes suggested). The guidelines offered in the eighth chapter or step in Life Mapping project, "Sharing My Life Story in a Supportive Group," should offer adequate details for putting together session plans and a workable schedule. The option is offered of incorporating this important sharing of Life Maps in the regular scheduled sessions or agreeing to a Saturday or weekend retreat format for completing this.

A Final Celebration Richard Peace's guide *Spiritual Autobiography: Discovering & Sharing Your Spiritual Story* stresses the importance of this final celebrative meeting and offers excellent suggestions for structuring it. After each group member has had the opportunity to share his or her Life Map with affirmation and blessing from members, this final session will almost plan itself. The bonds formed in some of my Spiritual Formation classes, the group in which a Life Map was shared, became life-long friendships. This is a "good-bye" session, but many of my groups had annual reunions and later get-togethers to keep in touch ad report progress since sharing Life Maps. The leader should honestly reflect the impact that this learning experience has had on him or her as part of the celebration. The leader might also mention any efforts he or she has taken to add a new chapter to a Life Map, and ways that may have helped to navigate a recent life transition. Encouragement for each member to use the Life Mapping project to creatively work through future hinge events, positive or negative, can be an important part of this last session. Seal this meeting with a prayer and blessing for the future.

Sources Mentioned

Chapter 1

- Doctor in Ministry thesis project by Rev. Noel Sherry, "Life Mapping as a Means of Redemptive Transformation: Change the Name and the Story is About You." Bethel University, St. Paul, MN, May 2017.
- Saint Augustine's classic spiritual autobiography *Confessions*, translated by Henry Chadwick (NY: Oxford University Press (1992).
- Journal article by Robert Butler, "The Life Review: An Interpretation of Reminiscence in the Aged," *Journal of Interpersonal Processes in Psychiatry* 28 (1963): 67-68.
- Book by Erich Auerbach, *Mimesis: The Representation of Reality in Western Literature* (Garden City, NY: Doubleday Anchor Books, 1953), 14-15.
- Journal article by Robyn Fivush, "Remembering and Reminiscing: How Individual Lives are Constructed in Family Narratives," *Memory Studies* 1, no. 1 (2008): 55.

Chapter 2

- Robert J. Havighurst's book *Human Development and Education* (NYC: Longmans Green & Co, 1957), 7.
- Richard Peace's guide titled *Spiritual Journaling: Recording Your Journey Toward God* (Colorado Springs, CO: NavPress, 1998).
- Dan McAdam's 1995 "Life Story Interview" (https://fliphtml5.com/kycl/gvku/basic).

Chapter 3

- Richard Peace's guide titled *Spiritual Journaling: Recording Your Journey Toward God* (Colorado Springs, CO: NavPress, 1998).
- Ira Progoff's award-winning *At a Journal Workshop: Writing to Access the Power of the Unconscious and Evoke Creative Ability* (NY, New York: Tarcher Perigee Publishing, 1992).

Chapter 4

- Book by Leland Ryken *How to Read the Bible as Literature…and Get More Out of It* (Grand Rapids, MI: Zondervan Publishing, 1984), pp. 80-81.
- Book by James Sire titled *The Universe Next Door: A Basic Worldview Catalog* (Downers Grove, IL: InterVarsity Press, 3rd Edition 1997).

- Article by Robert Coleman. "Creating a Life Story: The Task of Reconciliation." *The Gerontologist* 39, no. 2 (1999): 133-39.

Chapter 5

- Book by Ronald G. Smith titled *J. G. Hamann* (NYC: Harper and Brothers, 1960), 28.
- Northrop Frye's book *The Great Code: The Bible & Literature* (NYC: Harvest Books, 1982), 33.
- Book by Craig G. Bartholomew and Michael W. Goheen, *The Drama of Scripture: Finding Our Place in the Biblical Story* (Grand Rapids: Baker Academic Books, 2004), 27.
- Article by Robert M. Brown, "My Story and 'The Story'" in *Theology Today* 32 (1975): 166-173.
- Article by P. L. Hammack titled "Narrative and the Cultural Psychology of Identity" in *Personality and Social Psychology Review 12* (2008): 222–247.

Chapter Six

- American Psychiatric Association's definition of PTSD from its website https://www.psychiatry.org/patients-families/ptsd/what-is-ptsd
- B. K. Haight's article "Reminiscing: The State of the Art as a Basis for Practice," in *The Meaning of Reminiscence and Life Review,* ed. J. Hendricks (Amityville, NY: Baywood Publishing, 1995), 51-2.
- Peter Kreeft & Ron Tacelli's *Handbook of Christian Apologetics: Hundreds of Answers to Crucial Questions* (Downers Grove, IL: InterVarsity Press, 1994), p. 138.
- Article by Robert Coleman. "Creating a Life Story: The Task of Reconciliation" in *The Gerontologist* 39, no. 2 (1999): 133-39.
- Sam Rima & Gary McIntosh's book *Overcoming the Darkside of Leadership: The Paradox of Personal Dysfunction* (Grand Rapids, MI: Baker Books, 1997), p. 22.
- Richard Peace's guide titled *Spiritual Journaling: Recording Your Journey Toward God* (Colorado Springs, CO: NavPress, 1998), p. 46.

Chapter Seven

- Amy Mandelker & Elizabeth Power's *Pilgrim Souls: A Collection of Spiritual Autobiographies* (New York, NY: Touchstone Books, 1999), Blaise Pascal's "Memorial" is included on pp. 421-22.
- James Dillon's article titled "Psychology and Spiritual Life Writing" in *The Humanistic Psychologist* 39 (2011): 137-53.
- Dan Greenberg & Barb Knowlton's research article "The Role of Visual Imagery in Autobiographical Memory," in *Memory Cognition* 42:922-934 (2014).
- Richard Peace's guidebook *Spiritual Autobiography: Discovering & Sharing Your Spiritual Story* (Colorado Springs, CO: NavPress, 1998), pp. 82-83.

Chapter Eight

- Book by Richard Peace titled *Spiritual Autobiography: Discovering & Sharing Your Spiritual Story* (Colorado Springs, CO: NAV Press, 1998).

Chapter Nine

- Doctor in Ministry thesis project by Rev. Noel Sherry, "Life Mapping as a Means of Redemptive Transformation: Change the Name and the Story is About You" (Bethel University, St. Paul, MN, May 2017.
- Saint Augustine's classic spiritual autobiography, *The Confessions,* translated by Maria Boulding (Hyde Park, NY: New City Press, 1997). Confessions is divided by Book, Paragraph, and Line (1.1.1).
- William C. Spengemann's *The Forms of Autobiography: Episodes in the History of a Literary Genre* (New Haven, CT: Yale University Press, 1980).
- David M. Alberts doctoral project titled "Seeking My Face: Spiritual Autobiography and Truth" (Wesley Theological Seminary, 2004), p. 61.
- Dan McAdam's 1995 "Life Story Interview" questions (https://fliphtml5.com/kycl/gvku/basic).

Chapter Ten

- Richard Peace's guide titled *Spiritual Autobiography: Discovering & Sharing Your Spiritual Story* (Colorado Springs, CO: NavPress, 1998), p. 58.
- Elizabeth Jarrett Andrew's website on spiritual memoir, what it is, and examples of its practice-- https://www.spiritualmemoir.com/spiritual-memoir/what-is-spiritual-memoir.
- *A Family Genogram Workbook* by Israel Galindo, Elaine Boomer, and Don Reagan (www.galindoconsultants.com, 2006) is an excellent resource for understanding the emotional and spiritual context of one's family system and genealogy.

An Update with Helps for the Leader of a Life Map Group

- Richard Peace's guide titled *Spiritual Autobiography: Discovering & Sharing Your Spiritual Story* (Colorado Springs, CO: NavPress, 1998), pp. 53-54.

Printed in the United States
by Baker & Taylor Publisher Services